THE MOON IN T

A Carl Jung Coloring Book
for Self-Exploration

By Annette Poizner, M.S.W.

"Thus all the past is abandoned: for one day the herd might become master and drown all time in shallow waters. Therefore, O my brothers, a new nobility is needed to be the adversary of all mob rule and despotism and to write again the word 'noble' on new tablets."

Nietzsche, *Thus Spoke Zarathustra*

THIS BOOK BELONGS TO ME,

_____

(A WORK IN PROGRESS)

SELF-CREATION

"WHO AM I?

"Through pride we are ever deceiving ourselves. But deep down below the surface of the average conscience a still, small voice says to us, something is out of tune."

— Carl Gustav Jung

What is the question of greatest significance? Aldous Huxley nailed it: "Who am I? And what is to be done about it?"

Indeed, tracking the news these days, many hot button issues take us to the address of identity. If Carl Jung were here, he would be concerned.

Jung understood: healthy identity is essential for life success. Further, difficulties clarifying and establishing a healthy identity fuel a herd mentality. People would rally for causes, adopting narrow identities, pseudo-identities, failing to bring the full bandwidth of Selfhood forward. Sadly, many today are locked in this lifestyle.

Jung urged people away from movements and campaigns, ushering them, instead, inwards. And, he would say, it's not so easy to get 'buy in'. Jung reflected,

"Small and hidden is the door that leads inward, and the entrance is barred by countless prejudices, mistaken assumptions, and fears. Always one wishes to hear of grand political and economic schemes, the very things that have landed every nation in a morass. Therefore it sounds grotesque when anyone speaks of hidden doors, dreams, and a world within.

What has this vapid idealism got to do with gigantic economic programs, with the so-called problems of reality?"

Jung urged us to resist the pull to change the world, understanding that the true activist is the one who has first changed him or herself. Jung wrote:

"it goes without saying that cultural values do not drop down like manna from heaven, but are created by the hands of individuals. If things go wrong in the world, this is because something is wrong with the individual, because something is wrong with me. Therefore, if I am sensible, I shall put myself right first. For this I need . . . a knowledge of the innermost foundations of my being, in order that I may base myself firmly in the eternal facts of the human psyche."

I have prepared this set of coloring books to make the internal facts of the human psyche available, especially to those who do not normally read psychology tomes. We will see: Jung's central insights about identity, his understandings of the constituent parts of the psyche are very accessible. If the motto, 'a picture tells a million words' has any truth to it, we may find that the use of illustration helps drive home the elegance and validity of his insights.

Expect to discover Individuation, also the need to avoid falling into "unconsciousness," or group think. As Jung liked to to say, "thinking is difficult. It's easier to judge."

His goal is to awaken us to that which is unique, personal and essential within our own natures. If we have gotten swept up in ideologies, he wants to help release us. Jung's hope is that you will awaken, you will be one who "lights a hopeful watchfire announcing to others that at least one man has succeeded in escaping from the fateful identity with the group soul."

I have assembled these materials for you to dabble with Jungian psychology. In this volume, expect to learn Jung's most significant concepts relative to the Self and its component parts. Coloring mandalas will help you integrate these ideas and will also engage the dreaming mind. Use each book

to record the dreams that are stimulated when working with this material.

n Volume 2, you will engage with an exercise designed to help you explore and clarify, also expand, your current identity. Jung would routinely ask his patients" "What myth are you living?" Since, today, few know the ancient myths, we will access the archetypes by delving into nature. The animals represent the wide range of personality traits and archetypes. Set out to discover which animals are avatars for the traits and patterns that are uniquely yours. We will find ourselves in certain animals, not in others. Working with that volume will allow you to assess your personality style, also to garner insights into which areas, traits or animals represent needed areas for growth and development. Expect interesting surprises as you use a different lens to take stock of who you are and what you are like. The animals bring us home to our 'animal nature'.

Onward. We will look at why coloring is a worthwhile and helps us improve concentration skills. We will look at some of the core ideas that constitute a most important psychology and one that you might not access in the course of the usual day-to-day studies. We will explore the ideas of Carl Jung, often turning to his own words as he so wisely captures nuggets of truth about the human condition. Welcome to the interior universe! Come on home.

Annette Poizner, MSW, Ed.D., RSW
www.ap.annettepoizner.com

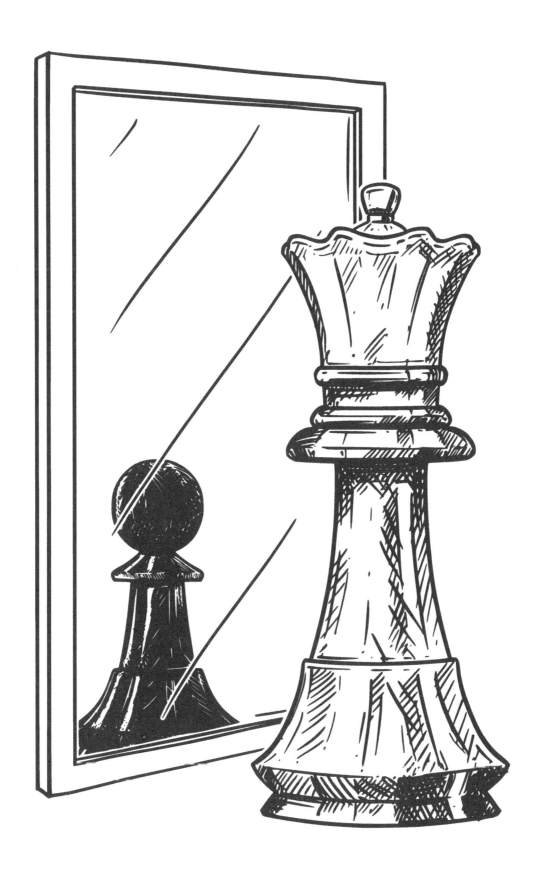

"The images of the unconscious place a great responsibility upon a man. Failure to understand them, or a shirking of ethical responsibility, deprives him of his wholeness and imposes a painful fragmentariness on his life."
Carl Jung

WHY COLOR?

In his most recent book, *Beyond Order*, Jordan Peterson offers a reflection: as a child, he knew 'the contours and details' of his neighborhood - "all the back alleys, the cracks in the pavement, the shortcuts." In contrast, relative to where he has been living now - for decades - he has but the vaguest sense of the other houses on his block. A busy life commands his attention,. He lacks a rich awareness of landmarks near at hand.

Peterson says, "I am simply not there in my adult neighborhood the same way I was as a child in my hometown." Perhaps you know what he means.

For Peterson, this lack of awareness is not just a matter of nostalgia. He tells us that when our perceptions are weakened, when we are separated in this way from reality, from the world and maybe from ourselves, we are missing something; a very deep feeling of belonging, and maybe more.

Peterson's problem is ours, as well. Can we open the 'doors of perception' which seem hammered shut? The barrage of websites, feeds and tweets overwhelm us . . . when responsibilities and worries finally let up. And with all this, we fail to notice or process, only retain hazy and broad impressions, fail to see the flowers for the trees. Visual acuity becomes strictly the domain of artists. Something is lost. The act of coloring, though, can bring us back to our senses.

A few years ago, adult coloring books became popular. These books offered a view of our world as exquisitely detailed. I would suggest these books help bring into consciousness the nuance that exists in the world around us. Working with these books, ministering to each design, tending to each detail, requires the kind of single-focused concentration that digital technology has otherwise decimated.

In days of yore, the writing instrument was 'Yang', active, relative to the clean sheet of paper on which you would leave your imprint. Now each website, each e-mail, each tweet leaves its imprint . . . on *you*! *You* are the blank slate! They are '*Yang*', you are '*Yin*'! You bear the imprint . . . of marketers, corporations, ideologies. Spinning in a dizzying environment full of messages, your perception of yourself as a dynamic initiator is dwarfed. You become small.

Nicholas Carr, in his book, *The Shallows: What the Internet Is Doing to Our Brains*, tells us that the proliferation of digital technology has changed the ways our brains work. Gone is the capacity for what he calls "deep reading." Now, we scan. We skim.

How can we reclaim depth and, for that matter, a sense of our own agency/capacity to have an impact? It's time to pick up writing utensils. It's time to come back to basics. Coloring was your activity when you were at the gate, ready to embark on your adventure with literacy. Time to retrace your steps. We have all strayed far from who we need to be, relative to the task of cognitive processing. The only thing to do: back up. Start over.

And so I invite you to revisit the world of pens and markers, pictures, imagery. It worked back then. It can work again now. And now, our process can be informed by a worldview that can help us achieve cognitive *and* personal goals. The psychology of Carl Jung provides an interesting and rich context for our journey into color, texture . . . and the Self!

MANDALAS

Mandalas, circular geometric patterns that emerged from the Hindu and Buddhist traditions, were of great interest to Psychiatrist Carl Jung. In this book, let's look at central concepts Jung put forward. As well, we will color mandalas, which, according to Jung, symbolize the state of wholeness and represent the singular Self.

Freud did much to advance the field of psychology, but his influence also doused us in pathology, as a frame of reference. In contrast, Jung brought spiritual overtones to our study of the psyche. He introduced us to the disparate parts within and here we will explore complexes, archetypes, inner faculties like the Persona, the Personal Unconscious and the Collective Unconscious.

But Jung also introduced a Self, the repository of all those parts, a self within which all talents, potentials or other aspects of selfhood would be nested. The mandalas geometric design, characterized by symmetry and organized details was designed to represent – and resonate with – our own inner essence. The mandala represents the Higher Self, who we become if we will order and architect the disparate parts we find within so that they each assume a perfect place within the whole. The designs are meant to awaken a sense memory of the potential we all harbor.

As well, the mandala represents the ideal structure of society or even that of the world, at large. Imagine each person in society represented as one of the details represented in the mandala. Can we each find our rightful place in society/within the collective? When we find that place, we retain our unique identity but also participate optimally in the broader world.

Frederick Buechner charges each one of us to find the place where 'our deep gladness and the world's deep need, meet'. The mandala visually represents this ideal state, signifying a coming together of individuals in a way that simultaneously serves each, individually, and the whole, collectively. We each become a puzzle piece that snaps into place, so completing the design, allowing a pattern to emerge that previously existed only in the realm of potential. The actualized individual properly manifests and all are better, as a result.

When people come together in a way that serves the greater good, Jung would tell us: expect wonderful payoffs for individuals *and* for society: more synchronicity in life, better relationships, more positive emotions, more teamwork.

We, each of us, can become an organized complexity wherein the various parts of Self find their rightful place within the unity. We are to take direction from the mandala and, as we color them, we resolve to identify each component part we find within – character traits? Skills? Different selves we can become in one context or another? – and organize them so each inter-includes harmoniously with the others. The mandala, then, guides us in our Self-creation process.

What rewards can we hope to accrue if we will bring together the disparate parts of self and organize them into an inner unity? When we achieve this, feelings, thoughts and deeds converge around priorities. We become focused and productive. The different splintered selves that we usually and normally find within come together, creating a singular will. When we fail to achieve this unity, we experience inner conflict: ambivalence, agitation, depression, confusion and doubt, even self-sabotage.

The effect of unity is similar to an anchor in a sailboat. The anchor makes the boat more resilient, more balanced, less effected by waves and wind. As you color the mandalas, set your intention: you are architecting a vision of wholeness. You are reaching for a Self that lets you be in the moment, on one hand, and above the moment, on the other.

Not surprisingly, research shows that mandala drawing nurtures positive feelings, promotes well-being and eases negative feelings.

Our specific interest here, of course, is the project which has a person working toward psychological harmony: Can we locate, categorize and landscape the various parts within so they come together in a way that is organizing and centering? Can we learn about the different parts of the psyche as they have been articulated by Jung and gain self-insight while doing so? Can we track dreams while engaging in this study in order to experientially encourage what Jung called 'the individuation process'?

Exploring Jung's ideas will trigger a more active dream life (That is what working on this book did for me!). Leave this book on the night table, by the bed. Make an effort to write down the dreams that you wake up with, recording them in the dream journal at the end of this book. Capturing those dreams will allow you to look for patterns, symbols and archetypes that may become obvious. Let us explore the inner world as it has been mapped out by Dr. Carl Jung.

KABBALISTIC MEANDERINGS

My fascination with the work of Carl Jung derived from the amazing correspondence between his ideas and those of the Jewish mystical tradition. In fact, Jung himself claimed that an ancient Kabbalist, the Hasidic Rabbi Baer of Meseritz, known as the Great Maggid, taught ideas that were aligned with Jung's own insights. Does mysticism have insights to bring forward?

THE ALEPH BEIT

You have probably paid little attention to the sequence of letters as they appear in the English alphabet. Why would you? If the letters k, l, m appeared in the reverse sequence, would it matter?

Um. No.

The Hebrew language, though, is different. Each Hebrew letter is a pictograph. The shape of each letter represents a concept. The name of the letter alludes to the same concept. The numerical value of each letter also consistently relays meaning and takes us back to the root concept. Even the order of the letters as they appear in the alphabet will be significant.

In Hebrew, the letters *Kaf*, *Lamed* and *Mem* are equivalent to the English letters k, l, m. These Hebrew letters follow the same sequence as they do in English. They are the middle letters of the Hebrew alphabet and their placement is hardly random. Let's see what they tell us.

Each Hebrew letter, we said, represents a concept. The word *Kaf*, then, refers to the palms of hands or soles of feet. The number that corresponds to that letter is 20, all the fingers and the toes! Let's think of *Kaf* as the physical power of the body and the physical instincts. That letter is the first of the Hebrew word for 'liver' and represents the strength each gets from that foundational organ. The following letter, *Lamed*, is the first letter of the Hebrew word, *Lev*, or heart.

See the illustration. When you take two *Lamed's* and present them as mirror images, they form a heart! The word *Lev* is comprised of two letters. The second letter, the *Beit*, represents the number 2! Two *Lamed's* constitute the heart!

Notice the sequence of letters in our alphabet, then: the first letter just mentioned associates with the physical instincts of a person, the second letter mentioned represents the emotions. What have you got when you combine the instincts and the emotions? Those two letters together form the Hebrew word *kol*, 'all'. The Persona, comprised of instincts and emotions, possesses the feeling that it is the whole you, it is 'all' of you.

Figure 1: Here you see two Lamed's, one has been reversed. When we align them side by side we have a glyph that resembles the heart. What does Lamed mean? Lilmod means 'to educate'! The heart is the organ that requires a process of learning or training in order to achieve maturity!

What is the next letter in the sequence? *Mem*. This letter is the first letter of *moach*, another organ, the brain.

If you think about the sequence again, you realize that these letters occur in the sequence that corresponds with the normal sequence of human development. We awaken initially on the level of instinct and emotion, later, we activate the brain.

The letter *Lamed*, representing the emotions, is telling. Lamed means 'to learn'! We must landscape our emotions, we must tame them and educate ourselves so that the feeling self will quiet down. This imperative, then, is embedded in the order of letters within the Hebrew A*leph Beit!*

As mentioned, the first two letters form the word, 'all', but the three letters together form other words, depending on how the letters are vowelized: *kloom* in Hebrew means 'nothing', *kalem* means 'annihilate' and *kulam* means 'everybody or everyone'. If a person lives in a way that instincts form emotions which then shape thoughts, a person becomes a member of the herd. The self has been annihilated. The 'all' of *kol* becomes the 'nothing' of *kloom*!

A person needs to do the work, to change the initial dominance where instinct leads, reversing things so that the brain becomes dominant. After all, those letters also form the word, *kaylim*, or tools. These primary organs and capacities are our tools! When we master them, and make the brain sovereign over the others, we now have a new word: *melech*, or King! Note, though, the letters are now in the reversed order!!

And this is what Carl Jung is telling us! We need to reclaim sovereignty, we need to bring insight and awareness, activating the brain and assuming its leadership over more instinctual aspects of the self. She who goes against the grain, reversing the direction that is natural but not necessarily evolved will achieve sovereignty, self-possession. As one more interesting aside, when the heart, Lev, is put in the first position, we have a new word: l*emach*, the fool!!

Jung asserts, "the one who distinguishes himself from the inescapable power of collectivity, thus freeing himself at least in the psychic way . . . lights a hopeful watchfire announcing to others that at least one man has succeeded in escaping from the fateful identity with the group soul." Here's to individuation!

What do we make of the fact that these three letters, bearing core messages that literally define the quality of life – sit smack in the middle of the Hebrew alphabet? The middle associates with the heart of the matter. Here's the message: the path of least resistance is conformity. The path to individuation – kingship – has us moving against the status quo, breaking from the herd and taking progressive steps in the right direction.

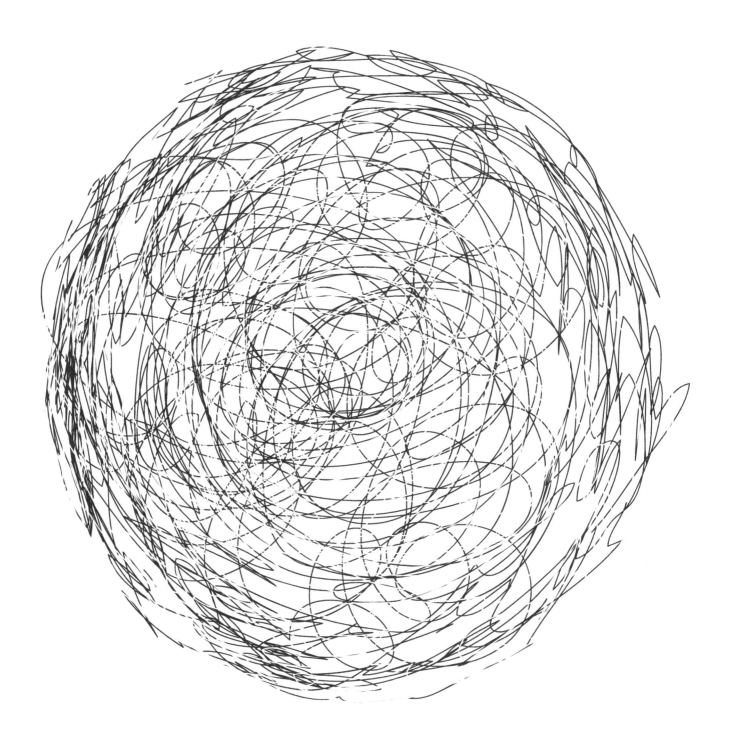

Your humble beginnings

Your ideal?

"Individualism means deliberately stressing and giving prominence to some supposed peculiarity."
Carl Jung

"Our aim is to create a wider personality whose center of gravity does not necessarily coincide with the ego, but which, on the contrary, may even thwart the ego-tendencies. Like a magnet, the new center attracts to itself that which is proper to it, the 'signs of the Father', namely everything that pertains to the original and unalterable character of the individual ground-plan.

Carl Jung

"People will do anything, no matter how absurd,
to avoid facing their own souls."
Carl Jung

"To find out what is truly individual in ourselves
profound reflection is needed;
and suddenly we realize how uncommonly difficult
the discovery of individuality in fact is."
Carl Jung

"...Man's consciousness was created to the end that it may recognize its descent from a higher unity; pay due and careful regard to this source; execute its commands intelligently and responsibly; and thereby afford the psyche as a whole the optimum degree of life and development."

Carl Jung

"Follow that will and that way
which experience confirms to be your own."
Carl Jung

"The privilege of a lifetime is to become
who you truly are."
Carl Jung

"I am what I choose to become."
Carl Jung

"The most terrifying thing
is to accept oneself completely."
Carl Jung

"... When all is said and done, our own existence is an experiment of nature, an attempt at a new synthesis."
Carl Jung, *Structure & Dynamics of the Psyche*

"The world will ask you who you are and if you don't know, the world will tell you."
Carl Jung

"Those who look outside, dream;
inside, awake."
Carl Jung

"In each of us there's another
who we do not know."
Carl Jung

"Every human life contains a potential. If that potential
is not fulfilled than that life was wasted."
Carl Jung

"Your vision will become clear only when you can look into your own heart."
Carl Jung

"A psychoneurosis must be understood as a soul which has not discovered its meaning."
Carl Jung

"If you will not reveal yourself to others, you cannot reveal yourself to yourself."
Jordan Peterson

"I will try to explain the term "individuation" as simply as possible.
By it I mean the psychological process that makes of a human being an
"individual" - a unique, indivisible unit or "whole man."
Carl Jung

"I am not what happened to me."
Carl Jung

"Strengthen the individual. Start with yourself. Take care of yourself. Define who you are. Refine your personality. Choose your destination."
Jordan Peterson

"You cannot aim yourself at anything if you are
completely undisciplined and untutored."
Jordan Peterson

"Don't tell yourself, "I shouldn't need to do that to motivate myself." What do you know about yourself? You are, on the one hand, the most complex thing in the entire universe, and on the other, someone who can't even set the clock on your microwave. Don't overestimate your self-knowledge."
Jordan Peterson

"There is an idea that all learning is remembering. You have a nature, and when you feel that nature articulated, it's like the act of snapping the puzzle pieces together."
Jordan Peterson

"What is it, in the end, that induces a man to go his own way and to rise out of unconscious identity with the mass as out of a swathing mist?
It is what is commonly called vocation: an irrational factor that destines a man to emancipate himself from the herd and from its well-worn paths. ... Anyone with a vocation hears the voice of the inner man: he is called."
Carl Jung

"You are a loose unity of a multiplicity of spirits many of which are doing their own thing and you are striving to bring them all to some form of unity."
Jordan Peterson

THE SELF

Channeling Jordan Peterson, let's start with the idea that classic fairytales and movies often encode mythic themes. Those themes can transform a simple rhyme so that it becomes a cultural icon.

An example? People of all ages can recite *Humpty Dumpty* verbatim. Why? Humpty, his wall, the horses, the men . . . ho-hum, really. The message is basic. The rhyming scheme, simple. Surely there are children's poems more worthy of attention? And yet, *Humpty Dumpty* is easily recited by the three-year-old and the 93-year-old. Go figure.

What about *Rock-A-Bye Baby?* Imagine serenading your infant about the fate of a child whose cradle, suspended in the trees, falls, resulting . . . in concussion? Broken bones? Death? Who would sing such a song?

And yet these verses are still on people's lips. Why? Because they point to an implicit truth, relevant now as we introduce some premises of Jung's analytic psychology.

Jung proposed the existence of a Higher Self, a composite of the various internal parts of you that constellate together to compose the broad, complex and multifaceted person that you are. Each person will find many aspects within – even little subpersonalities – but, says Jung, an overarching Self encapsulates all the parts.

For Jung, it was a priority to discover that Self or to grow into it, a priority to push beyond more constricted, narrow states of being so as to incarnate a more resilient, more wise and more actualized and singular you.

What does this have to do with Humpty?

Jung was influenced by spiritual wisdom traditions. Many traditions hold that in utero, the Self is expansive. Socrates asserted that prior to birth, the self harbors all knowledge which it loses, upon birth. The Jewish tradition echoes this idea. The Talmud teaches: in utero the infant learns all wisdom, taught by an angel. When labor begins, the tradition holds, the angel gives the baby a blow right above the mouth. The result: amnesia! The baby remembers nothing. Now a blank slate, the self has a lifetime to reclaim the lost knowledge; also, to regain aspects of Self that were fractured and displaced at birth.

Enter *Humpty Dumpty* and *Rock-A-Bye Baby*. These verses tell us that birth is the ultimate fall from grace. We sing these songs to babies who have suffered loss of the ideal environment. We acknowledge the loss. Consciousness is now fractured, paradise lost. We teach *Humpty Dumpty*, we sing *Rock-A-Bye Baby*, because these verses acknowledge the fall. That seamless and endless Self has taken a hit. The child will now find many selves within, some out of conscious awareness, many at odds with best set agendas, fueling chaos, as a result.

And the King, representing the authorities? Parents? Government? Whatever established unity reigns in society at this point in time? The King simply cannot help here. We are each on our own.

Deal with it. That's life.

Jung introduced the priority of reclaiming this expansive Self. He articulated some of the faculties that we find within it. In this way, he serves as a tour guide, pointing the path forward. We *can* know the constituent parts within. We can retain an understanding of the full breadth of the Self realizing the ego is *not* the one and only Self. Jung teaches: the Persona deceives us. It would have us believe that *it is* the Self. We must look past it to find a greater personality, broader, more expansive. Also, more hidden from view.

Douglas Hofstadter writes, "the soul is more than the hum of its parts." If that is true, then we have to explore the various aspects within so we can get that soul humming along nicely. Jung wants us to cultivate a unity, integrating all the parts we find within and even details how that might be achieved. Let's tour the psyche, get to know the real estate so we can develop the Self, with his guidance. It's time to landscape the interior - aka 'interior design'!

CONSCIOUS & UNCONSCIOUS

Not unlike Freud, Jung conceptualized two aspects of the psyche: the conscious and the unconscious. In common parlance, we often think of them as corresponding to the left brain and the right brain, respectively. In fact, the idea that these faculties are perfectly localized in this way is unlikely. On the other hand, there are some correspondences stand. Evidence locates the ability to analyze pieces of information, in isolation, with the left brain.

For Jung, the conscious self was the home base of everyday consciousness, allowing us to navigate the problems of the present and the demands of the external world. The conscious self would be the arbiter of the present, possessing a day-to-day awareness of self and other, analyzing the details of life.

Jung emphasized, though, that the Persona, the ego/self with which we comfortably identify, is a marauder. It radiates the sense that *it* is the overarching self. In calling this conscious self the Persona, Jung implies it's way of being has been shaped by the expectations of others, thereby masking the true Self.

We are told that much growth is achieved by dipping into deeper aspects of selfhood. How? Through self-exploration and by analyzing dreams.

With regard to the various faculties within: when they function autonomously, without sharing content, the result: neurosis. The ideal state has us moving content from one part of the mind to the others. There should be a degree of integration between them.

Let's consider an example: imagine a person remains unaware of his or her intrinsic artistic ability which is harbored within the unconscious. This latent talent can be cultivated *if* the conscious self comes to know about the talent harbored within. Unpacking the inner reservoir brings more richness into life and allows a person to know themselves better and to express themselves in new ways.

Of course, beyond positive attributes we find within, we also find neuroses or personal issues. Jung suggests that if we delve into the contents of the unconscious we will potentially resolve mental health difficulties and promote growth and self-insight.

Our next task is to look at some of the faculties that we find within.

THE UNCONSCIOUS MIND

Let's return to *Humpty Dumpty*. It's interesting: Humpty has been represented as an egg in drawings . Is the large oval represented in that rhyme really an egg? Could it more realistically be a head with a face, representing the part of the human body we associate with singularity and identity? That would make sense, When we see the face and the head of another, this particular body part embodies, for us, the identity of the person. Yet, we earlier came to the conclusion that the one head/one face aspect of the human body, is misleading.

Within each person, there are many selves. Each person is fragmented and thereby initially prone to ambivalence, inner conflict, confusion. Perhaps *Humpty Dumpty* relays a quiet truth: we may start off as a unity, then we each splinter into a multiplicity. We look like a unity, we want to be a unity, but we ain't.

Even the King, his horses, his men – all his constituent aspects – are stymied by the plurality that is you. They can't help.

And don't take it personally. It's true about everyone else, as well. We are all variable. No wonder we have moods, symptoms, or a tendency to get pulled in different directions. Jung orients you, providing a way to look at and understand some of the fragments you find within. He also guides you in the process of bringing the parts together and knitting them into a unity. Let's see what else we find within.

THE PERSONAL UNCONSCIOUS

Lurking beyond the Persona in the deeper realms of consciousness, Jung located the personal unconscious. Within this faculty we find aspects of self out of reach of day-to-day awareness. This faculty is also the address of complexes and complexities, personal issues that may fuel symptoms or neuroses, beliefs or memories that may retain the emotional charge of yesteryear: all of these may influence your lifestyle in a way that may be counterproductive.

The personal unconscious harbors much of the hidden mystery of the psyche. Like Freud, Jung believed that the content of the personal unconscious was necessarily of interest in therapy. By deciphering issues and complexes, the Persona would gradually confront and integrate aspects of Self, re-engaging those parts that had been splintered off and hidden within. Doing so would expand the self-concept, adding breadth and depth to the day-to-day experience of consciousness.

Perhaps it was this process that was alluded to by Poet Rainer Rilke when he wrote,

"I am learning to see. I don't know why it is, but everything penetrates more deeply into me and does not stop at the place where until now it always used to finish. I have an inner self of which I was ignorant. Everything goes thither now. What happens there I do not know."

ANIMA/ANIMUS

Another facet of the personal unconscious is the Anima/Animus. In Genesis, describing the creation of man, the Bible reads, "Masculine & Feminine, He created them." This creation account, therefore, attests : humans possess a masculine *and* feminine aspect. Jung, in advancing his model, was putting forward a notion that dates back to antiquity.

Jung suggested that a woman possessed a masculine aspect which contained her own allotment of traits, associated with the *Yang* dimension, in the language of Chinese philosophy. These traits include assertiveness, decisiveness, analytical thought, desire for achievement and capacity for focus on tasks. This aspect of the unconscious, called the Animus, would be modelled after male figures in her past, likely her father. For a man, his Anima would govern his capacity to connect with others, and also shape his experience of emotions. His Anima would be modelled after his mother or other important female influences.

The woman's Animus would dictate particularities about her love interests, the types of character traits that would attract her, and would also dictate the nature of her interest in the world of ideas or rationality, more generally. Male influences in her earlier life would color her expectations, associations and preferences relative to the 'masculine' domain.

Similarly, a man's Anima would influence his emotional patterns and his choice of love interest, priming him toward people whose traits resembled those of early female influences.

For Jung, the Anima and the Animus, for the male and female, respectively, was a bridge to the unconscious mind, the gateway to a part of the self that was necessarily less-developed but would individuate over time. In fact, to the degree a person extends forth and develops the Self is the degree to which they unpack and develop the Anima or Animus.

We necessarily need to integrate this part, to master its proper expression in the world and to properly integrate it into the personality. In fact, in the case of physical development, men and women, as they age, experience hormonal shifts. They become, effectively, more androgynous. Women's testosterone levels elevate and estrogen is diminished. Men accrue higher levels of estrogen and testosterone diminishes. Just as the body of the aging male or female comes into a new balance relative to male and female traits, so too, each must evolve psychologically.

In the latter part of life, after middle age, each person would cultivate more mastery of the traits which were less-developed, initially. A man might work to master the traits of relatedness associated with his Anima and a woman might master her rational faculties, associated with her Animus.

Within the personal unconscious, we find complexes, the Shadow and also the Anima/Animus. Let's explore further.

COMPLEXES

Taking a deeper look at complexes, brings us face-to-face with residues or impacts from moments in our lives where we were triggered. Complexes are points of intensity which constellate around a theme, issue or idea that is emotionally charged, tripping us into positive or negative emotions. The negative complexes can trigger reactivity and awaken old states, unhappy narratives from yesteryear.

Psychologist Jordan Peterson prescribes journal writing which people can use to gain self-insight and to identify their complexes. Peterson's research shows that doing his extensive journaling project bears fruit. First year university students who used it, in the context of a research study, had a lower dropout rate and achieved higher marks than the control group, consisting of students who didn't do the journaling.

THE SHADOW

For Jung, one important faculty within the personal unconscious is the Shadow. Jung conceptualized the Shadow as the repository of aspects of the self that people disown. These may be parts of the self which were met with disapproval by parents or authority figures, part of the dark side that each person necessarily possesses or part of the self that doesn't match the individual's preferred Persona.

Take for example a woman who knows herself to be warm and friendly. Her shadow might bear aggression, out of sight, out of mind, but necessarily part of the inner infrastructure since each person has such a faculty. If she is uncomfortable with her own aggressive impulses, she may repress them so they remain locked out of awareness.

Carl Jung asserted: "that which we resist, persists." When a part of the self is disowned it lurks in the unconscious but, without being properly integrated into day-to-day consciousness, it potentially activates neurotically and produces symptoms. Or it attaches to people out there who possess the 'hated' quality, and these people/this group becomes the scapegoat, justifying prejudice or negativity.

Jung would argue that if aspects of self are hidden in the wings, so to speak, they can cause disturbance. A process is then needed to bring the contents of the unconscious into consciousness. One way to achieve this: tracking dreams. The unconscious mind will dream about inner dynamics at play. When the conscious self explores and understands the complexities that have been locked away within, the repression often lifts and symptoms may disappear or gradually fade.

COLLECTIVE UNCONSCIOUS

If the personal unconscious of an individual harbors beliefs, complexes, and latent potentials, the Collective Unconscious harbors material that is common to all humanity. Analyzing dreams and myths, Jung realized that people were subject to influences that extended beyond their narrow lives or unique experiences. Certain recurrent themes would pepper the imagination of young and old, alike, producing recurrent themes. Jung identified many of these, referring to them as archetypes.

Across cultures or nationalities, he found certain roles or processes that seemed wired into the human psyche. People seem fixated on roles such as the hero or the victim, or processes such as birth or death, leading Jung to assume that they were all pivotal and that we had to enact them and manifest them while moving forward in life.

Jung would track the archetypes when interpreting dreams or fairytales. Others, such as Dr. Jordan Peterson, continue, to this day, to describe their import and use them in therapy. We can build courage by animating the Hero archetype or garner support by cultivating the Mother archetype. We can do life review exercises or analyze dreams to see which archetypes are dominant or deficient in our lives.

"Knowing your own darkness is the best
method for dealing with the darknesses of
other people."
— Carl Gustav Jung

"We have to discover our shadow.
Otherwise we are driven into a world war
in order to see what beasts we are."
Carl Jung

Visions: Notes of the Seminar Given in 1930 – 1934

"How can I be substantial if I don't cast a shadow?
I must have a dark side also if I am to be whole."
Carl Jung

"A man cannot get rid of himself in favour of an artificial personality without punishment. Even the attempt to do so brings on, in all ordinary cases, unconscious reactions in the form of bad moods, affects, phobias, obsessive ideas, back slidings, vices, etc."
Carl Jung

INDIVIDUATION

"The fact that a man who goes his own way ends in ruin means nothing ... He must obey his own law, as if it were a daemon whispering to him of new and wonderful paths ... There are not a few who are called awake by the summons of the voice, whereupon they are at once set apart from the others, feeling themselves confronted with a problem about which the others know nothing. In most cases it is impossible to explain to the others what has happened, for any understanding is walled off by impenetrable prejudices. "You are no different from anybody else," they will chorus or, "there's no such thing," and even if there is such a thing, it is immediately branded as "morbid"...He is at once set apart and isolated, as he has resolved to obey the law that commands him from within. "His own law!" everybody will cry. But he knows better: it is the law...The only meaningful life is a life that strives for the individual realization — absolute and unconditional— of its own particular law ... To the extent that a man is untrue to the law of his being ... he has failed to realize his own life's meaning."
— Carl Jung

"The frightened individual seeks for somebody or something to tie his self to; he cannot bear to be his own individual self any longer, and he tries frantically to get rid of it and to feel security again by the elimination of this burden: the self."
— Erich Fromm, *Escape from Freedom*

"When one has let go of that great hidden agenda that drives humanity and its varied histories, then one can begin to encounter the immensity of one's own soul. If we are courageous enough to say, "Not this person, nor any other, can ultimately give me what I want; only I can," then we are free to celebrate a relationship for what it can give."
— James Hollis, *Eden Project: In Search of the Magical Other*

"Jung called this process I'm describing individualism, becoming an individual, a real person not continually swept away by his passions or influenced by his culture. Each person has a unique opus, a soul work, because each has a particular makeup and history. For Jung the opus was a process of getting to know yourself deeply, not only a psychological process of painful advance in self-knowledge; but a religious initiation involving spiritual ideals and the search for meaning."
— Thomas Moore, *A Religion of One's Own: A Guide to Creating a Personal Spirituality in a Secular World*

POSSESSION

Beyond conjecturing about the specific parts that constitute the Self, Jung introduced ideas about the ways these parts function when they are well integrated, compared to their function when they are rejected, avoided or subject to negative impacts in response to trauma.

For example, in men and women, healthy masculinity animates rational thinking and motors abilities like goalsetting and task execution. Healthy femininity in men and women will translate into a good ability to relate with others and a healthy capacity to experience emotions.

When, though, people have blocks or complexes which impede healthy masculinity, (by way of example), the expression of masculinity will likely be contorted, interfering with rational thought. In the worst case, the 'masculinity' within invades the ego, causing the person to fixate on ideas that relate to personal complexes. The person infuses every conversation with inappropriate dialogue, misapplying ideas, obsessively advancing them in ways others experience as irrational.

Jung famously said, "people don't have ideas. Ideas have people." When the masculine essence is not properly developed nor integrated, the person becomes belligerent, forcefully putting forward ideas and misapplying them. When this trend becomes rampant, ideologies spread like a catchy virus.

Relative to the feminine aspect, if there are difficulties properly animating the feminine, the result may be a feminine archetype that intrusively dominates. That person becomes encumbered by moods and reactivity. It's as if another self, a splinter self, boots up and takes over, when triggered.

This invasion can occur relative to any archetype or even any personality trait. As Alexander Dumas wrote, "Any virtue, in excess, becomes a crime." If the archetype of home is properly animated, a person is home wherever they go. They will take good care of themselves, making the body a pleasant home. If there is a complex, perhaps a negative history with mother, past trauma or some other cause, a person may never leave home, so dominant is the nesting instinct.

Any archetype can be a progressive part of the self when integrated, or a source of disturbance, otherwise. Jung noted that the way to protect oneself from falling into destructive ideologies was to examine and deconstruct complexes and prioritize individuation. Properly bringing the self to fruition keeps a person from succumbing to ideologies that take the world by storm, thereby staving off the cognitive version of a virus. Only through self-development can we ensure that the social fabric will be strong and viable. We need a societal commitment to personal development for individuals *and* we also need a frame of unity consciousness to prevail. We must value personal integration *and* social harmony. Both lead to wholeness.

"The convictions one has about oneself are the most subtle form of persona and the most subtle obstacle against any true individuation. One could admit practically anything, yet somewhere one retains the idea that one is nevertheless so-and-so, and this is always a sort of final argument which counts apparently as a plus; yet it functions as an influence against true individuation.

It is a most painful procedure to tear off those veils, but each step forward in psychological development means just that, the tearing off of a new veil. We are like onions with many skins, and we have to peel ourselves again and again in order to get at the real core."

Carl Jung, *Visions: Notes of the Seminar given in 1930 – 1934, Volume II*

"Every form of addiction is bad, no matter whether the narcotic be alcohol, morphine or idealism."
— Carl Jung

"Small and hidden is the door that leads inward, and the entrance is barred by countless prejudices, mistaken assumptions, and fears. Always one wishes to hear of grand political and economic schemes, the very things that have landed every nation in a morass. Therefore it sounds grotesque when anyone speaks of hidden doors, dreams, and a world within. What has this vapid idealism got to do with gigantic economic programmes, with the so-called problems of reality?

But I speak not to nations, only to the individual few, for whom it goes without saying that cultural values do not drop down like manna from heaven, but are created by the hands of individuals. If things go wrong in the world, this is because something is wrong with the individual, because something is wrong with me. Therefore, if I am sensible, I shall put myself right first. For this I need – because outside authority no longer means anything to me – a knowledge of the innermost foundations of my being, in order that I may base myself firmly in the eternal facts of the human psyche."

Carl Jung, *The Meaning of Psychology for Modern Man*

INDIVIDUATION

In the Jewish tradition, the plight of the soul as it moves through life is likened to a boat at sea. The boat represents the body/self which, moving through life, will be naïve of its context: oceanic oneness. Just as a fish, so immersed, does not know the water it inhabits, so, too, we remain fundamentally unaware of that context, the (hidden) warp and woof of existence.

Earlier, I described the task of self-exploration, mining the nooks and crannies of the personal unconscious and making the contents conscious; I talked about the impact of undertaking this sort of self-exploration process, likening it to the effect of dropping the anchor of a sailboat. That anchor has a dropped line attached, a line that embodies the shape of the number one, a straight line, signifying the singular identity that has been achieved, once inner turmoil is resolved. As complexes are diffused, as the inflated ego is gradually deflated, as the anima or animus is integrated, there is more maturity, more peacefulness, more clarity. The state we are working to achieve may be the one that has been described by Emerson when he wrote:

"Standing on the bare ground – my head bathed by the blithe air and uplifted into infinite space – all mean egotism banishes. I become a transparent eyeball; I am nothing; I see all; the currents of the Universal Being circulate through me; I am part or parcel of God."

Or perhaps the ideal state we strive to embody is that articulated in the ancient Chinese text, " The Large Discourse"):

In that the person becomes like the heavens and the earth, he does not come to be opposed to them. His wisdom embraces all things and his mind orders the whole world. Because of this, he does not make any mistakes. He has an effect on everything, but he does not let himself be carried away by anything. He is joyful of the heavens and knows fate. Thus, he is free of worries. He is satisfied with his situation and sincere in his goodness. Therefore, he is capable of expressing love (as quoted in Eckert, 1996, p. 29).

At the end of the day, we aspire to move away from the various states that signify arrested development; bland conformity or chaotic rebellion as two noteworthy examples, polar opposites, at that. When the individual cultivates a unified existence there is a merging of 'who I am' with 'what I do'. Those two unite, the coming together of noun and verb, self and mission.

For many decades, I've been a graphologist, a counsellor who derives tentative insights about individuals by examining their handwriting. I've written elsewhere about this interesting practice, but here I'd like to present signatures as a means of graphically illustrating one way that identity is expressed. Since this book relies on the visual medium, handwriting seems an interesting complement, especially the study of signatures. When penning a signature, a person produces a visual moniker to represent his or her identity. Given our focus on identity and its formation, examining signatures seems a fitting foray.

SIGNATURE GALLERY

Let's review some signatures so we can come up with some tentative insights. Of course, all of this takes us to the realm of conjecture but we can explore what the field of graphology might put forward.

Jane Russell

Remember Jane Russell? She was a pinup girl/movie star in the 1950s. Her signature trait (quite literally) was her buxom appearance. Looking at her signature, the graphologist sees convention and conformity as indicated by a copybook script that conforms loyally to the copybook script she would have learned in school. Handwriting is usually adapted by writers so that they modify the copybook style to integrate and accommodate their own individuality. The writer who chooses not to modify but to loyally reiterate the copybook is showing allegiance to classical values, revealing a traditionalist. Such a writer may be foregoing the call to individuation which requires self-exploration and expression

Note the inflation of the first letter of her last name (her professional name indicating her public self). Note the symbol. She embeds a glyph representing her famous swollen bust line, her claim to fame. Celebrity can block individuation. A woman celebrated for her looks may forego

individuation, never unpacking her depth, instead pandering to the eye of the camera.

Comedian Chris Rock's Signature

At the opposite end of the continuum, we see the signature of Chris Rock. Technically illegible, this signature expresses rebellion.

Writers have to find a point midway between conformity/convention and individuality/expression. Enough conformity is required so the writing will be legible. In producing a legible handwriting, the person is cooperating, aligning with the societal necessity to be clear and forthcoming. The writer who produces a legible writing which simultaneously expresses individuality is the person who individuates comfortably.

This particular writer contorts letter forms, defying the norm to produce a legible script and creates a signature that looks chaotic.

We hope that a signature will relay identity and live true to its task of identifying the unity of the person. Here, we don't find unity of purpose, a comfortable melding of self with the collective/society. This signature: contorted, fragmented letters in disarray. If Jane Russell's Persona writing shows hyper-conventional tendencies, her living up to the expectations of a society that venerated her looks, this writing seems to indicate a Persona which venerates rebellion.

Tiger Wood's signature

Finally, let's look at the signature of Tiger Woods. This is an interesting signature because if we consider it relative to both convention and individuality, we find both.

At first glance, this carefully penned signature looks, from a distance, to be legible and indicating a writer who conforms to expectations of legibility.

Look closer! Each letter is penned in an odd manner, and important details are omitted. Where is the crossing of the Capital *T*? Such an odd way to form a *g*, starting with the lower loop first! The handwriting seems planned, almost perfectionistic. And yet, since it is clearly penned very slowly, notice all the unusual adjustments that defy convention. The handwriting has the semblance of the copybook style of writing, looking conventional at first glance. Yet, with all these highly individualistic ways of forming letters, he is hardly conforming! He does things his own way! But he has an overall look about him, as if he quietly blends in and seemingly conforms, when, in actual fact, he is defiantly pursuing his own agendas and doing things his *own* way. The graphologist anticipates he is other than he appears!

The graphologist keeps looking and speculates about what may be imagery that seems embedded in the writing. See the 'sexy' W of his last name. That letter looks like a feminine body part. Notice a canopy of sorts that suspends above that erotic image as if hiding it from view? Since when would anyone create a letter form like *that? S*uch an unusual embellishment! Why is it there?

The graphologist might speculate sexual impropriety which is being shielded from view. Interestingly, this signature was penned about a year before his infidelity came to light. Is this relevant imagery that we find in the handwriting? Can't say for sure but Freud said, ""He that has eyes to see and ears to hear may convince himself that no mortal can keep a secret. If his lips are silent, he chatters with his fingertips; betrayal oozes out of him at every pore." People often embed imagery in handwriting that seems relevant. On that note, look at the last letter of his last name (representing Woods' public self). Do you see a putter?

While we are not assuming that handwriting can, in any way, provide a final word about a person and their psychology, our premise here is that people need to find a way to express themselves that partly conforms to societal norms while simultaneously expressing their unique individuality. We must neither be too conforming nor too rebellious. There is a centrist position that we are meant to pursue.

We've looked at some signatures of individuals who, at the time of writing, might have been challenged relative to the individuation journey. Now let's look at some signatures of those who might be role models, relative to the life task.

Lily Tomlin

Firstly I reproduce the handwriting of Comedian Lily Tomlin. Note the fluidity and flow in the sample. Creative embellishments add artistic flair. They serve legibility, never detracting. This writer shows healthy variability – using both angles and loops when constructing letters, yet there is a consistency in the writing – we feel a unity that radiates out a selfsameness. She has her own way about her. She's at home in her skin. Imagine that any handwriting has an energy or a feel to it. Here we see warmth, exuberance, life!

I find symbolism in this sample. See how a private little room is formed within which she pens the top stroke of the capital T? The large handwriting reveals a performer who hungers to be at the center of attention. The discrete little room which encases that sweeping horizontal straight line reveals a writer who also guards and maintains a private inner world. She who individuates, maintains a balance between all things.

Prime Minister Justin Trudeau's Signature

By way of contrast and comparison, let's segue to Justin Trudeau's signature. We see the large showy loops of the performer but legibility is lost and privacy strokes create busy lines encircled within protective capital letters. With script hidden within big loops that encircle, there is the connotation of secrets, hiddenness. This handwriting radiates showmanship but the identity is difficult to decipher. The graphologist conjectures that he hides much, out of sight. Newspaper reports would seem to confirm that this, indeed, is the case. With Lily Tomlin, though, what you see is what you get. There's her Persona and the private existence which is separate but both coexist, comfortably integrated into the broader self. And you can read what she writes.

Justin Trudeau's handwriting, according to the graphologist, implies a writer who plays to his audience and is hypervigilant about how he looks, the sign of the performer with the dominant Persona.

See the little glyph/cartoon character embedded in his signature which shows the profile of a man's face facing the right margin, cartoon eyes, nose, facing the right margin? This is a writer who watches us watching him. A few years before running for prime minister, he was passed a note, onboard a commercial flight. Someone had penned a message, asking whether he, indeed, was going to be the next Prime Minister of Canada. Trudeau passed the note back with three words: "Just watch me." This story reveals a psychology: he sees himself on stage being watched, as per that embedded symbol!

Astronaut Neil Armstrong's signature

Let's next look at the signature of Astronaut Neil Armstrong. Do you see, embedded in his signature, a rocket and a launchpad?

Take a look at the signature of Astronaut Sally Ride. In high school, she was working at becoming a tennis pro. One day she was in an adolescent funk and her father said:

"You can go to the stars!" His words stayed with her, she reported. When destiny speaks, we can hear it on a cellular level. In her case, the upward ascent was a calling. It found its expression in her career, her signature . . . . .and her life!

Karen Kain's signature

Look at the signature of Karen Kain, former Prima Ballerina and Artistic Director of the National Ballet of Canada. In her signature, we see two dancers, arm in arm, taking a bow at the end of the performance. Or could you see the two loops within the capital letters as footprints of her ballet slippers, laces hanging to the back of the shoes, representing steps taken as the dancer departs, stage left?

Frederick Buechner tells us to find the place where our gladness and the world's deep need meet. Don't be surprised when people shine out their life task in virtually anything they do, including handwriting!

Reflection Questions

What is my Persona like? How would people describe me?

What is my shadow - vices, flaws, undeveloped aspects?

What are my complexes/triggers?

How do I experience and express my Animus?

What aspects of my Self have I brought to fruition? What are new aspects I have to develop and bring forward?

Who are role models relative to the hard work of individuating?

For answers to these and other important questions, begin recording your dreams!

DREAM JOURNAL

"I HAD A DREAM!"

Use this journal to record dreams you wake up with as you work through the coloring book. Recording your dreams and reviewing them, you may find patterns emerge. Conversely, it is possible that you would need input from an experienced therapist to extract the specific meaning of your dreams. Either way – whether you garner insight from them or not – I'd like to suggest that much is achieved if you record your dreams.

On what basis do I make such a claim?

Let me point out a relevant fact and also a question: why is it that children's fairytales or movies so consistently advance supernatural scenarios? We have talking animals, machines that are alive, magic dragons and the like, just so much unreality. You might even imagine that these storylines are not unlike dreams, full of impossibilities which are presented as normative. Why would children's narratives consistently advance bizarre scenes, by reality standards?

We might get a partial insight if we consider how children acquire immunity. Faced with every germ, every virus, they struggle with each pathogen, ultimately acquiring a capacity, in so doing. Each exposure is a stretch. Similarly, we expose children to many shades of unreality which stretch and tone the imagination. By doing this, the creative imagination will become a conduit to mental health. We frequently assume that the creative disposition is a precursor to madness. But, as GK Chesterton notes

"The madman is not the man who has lost his reason. The madman is the man who was lost everything except his reason . . . . His mind moves in a perfect but narrow circle."

It turns out: rationality is one factor which contributes to mental health. Yet, there are other abilities that must be developed, simultaneously. Rationality allows us to discern and deconstruct reality. Yet, the imagination bench presses in a different way, helping us do important mental machinations. Thinking in all four directions, we can do pirouettes, leaping above and around the limitations of the actual, suspending ourselves in the realm of potential. Also, the imagination can sustain us in bleak moments, reminding us that inner resources can emerge unexpectedly and against all odds, helping us access mythic archetypes that can materialize in a moment's notice. The hero may gallop in and save the day! The elder may emerge with missing information! Miracles happen. The imagination doesn't have to predict the exact right remedy; it sustains us by creating hope and expectation, the implicit faith of transcendent forces which could activate at any moment.

For lack of imagination, a person becomes brittle. This is the person who never dreams. The path of self-exploration, then, requires us to landscape this part of the self. When we do, we develop a faculty that is our bridge to infinity. As Chesterton reflects in his book, *Orthodoxy*, "Poetry is sane because it floats easily in an infinite sea; reason seeks to cross the infinite sea, and so make it finite." The result: mental exhaustion. He adds, "To accept everything is an exercise, to understand everything a strain." Rationality gets us only so far. Imagination does its own version of heavy lifting though achieves this outcome easily, well suited for its job.

And so, you reaching into the irrational world, recording and examining the postcards sent by the active imagination when you awaken, is an elixir. Who said that it is only children who need a steady infusion of the irrational and other-worldly?

We bombard ourselves with the news, constantly reminding ourselves of current limitations. The economy is terrible. People's lives have been devastated by the events of the last two years. No mystery here. And yet, when we have no bridge to the realm of mystery, our troubles are even worse. Chesterton says, "As long as you have mystery you have health; when you destroy mystery you create morbidity. The ordinary man has always been sane because the ordinary man has always been a mystic. He is permitted the twilight. He has always had one foot on earth and the other in fairyland."

Being comfortable with both the tangible and intangible aspects of life, this is the person who can take nourishment from religion. Chesterton says about the one who hosts mystery, He has always left himself free to doubt his Gods; but (unlike

the agnostic of today) free also to believe in them." Not needing to resolve every doubt, able to host complexity and contradiction, Chesterton described this as the person with spiritual sight that is effectively stereoscopic: "he sees two different pictures at once and yet sees all the better for that." He adds:

"it is exactly this balance of apparent contradictions that has been the whole buoyancy of the healthy man. The whole secret of mysticism is this: that man can understand everything by the help of what he does not understand. The morbid logician seeks to make everything lucid, and succeeds in making everything mysterious. The mystic allows one thing to be mysterious, and everything else becomes lucid."

Your dreams, then, are an invitation into the realm of mystery, conjured by the part of self that has a foothold on the irrational. So many years ago, Fritz Perls urged his students to lose their minds and come to their senses. Carl Jung would urge us to loosen the exclusive hold we grant the rational mind and the Persona and to extend a hand to the part that brings offerings from the great beyond. I don't know the shifts you might experience by exerting in this direction – taking an active interest in dreams, writing them down and reviewing them. But I'd like you to find that out for yourself.

"In all chaos there is a cosmos, in all
disorder a secret order."
Carl Jung

"The interpretation of dreams is the royal road to a knowledge of the unconscious activities of the mind"
— Sigmund Freud, The Interpretation of Dreams

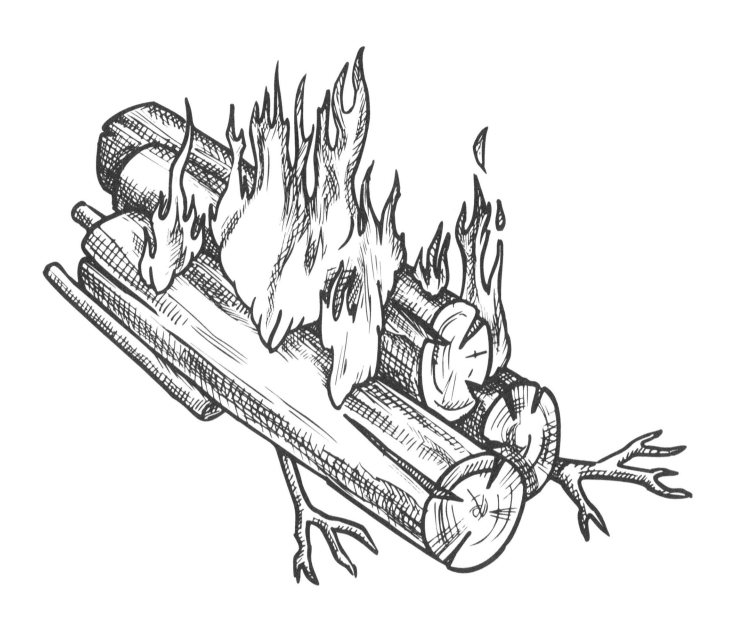

"Every transformation demands as its precondition "the ending of a world"-the collapse of an old philosophy of life."
— C.G. Jung, Man and His Symbols

CONSIDERING BIBLICAL ARCHETYPES

UNDERSTANDING BFF'S

On the 50th anniversary of the Mary Tyler Moore Show pilot, we recall the show that put a spotlight on the BFF - 'Best Female Friend' - relationship. Remember beautiful Mary, jealous Rhoda; conventional Mary, quirky Rhoda; beloved Mary, rejected Rhoda. In fact, you find a similar pairing in a more recent show, Grace and Frankie.

If you wondered whether there are classic archetypes at play when we watch a beautiful protagonist and her artistic, less polished, out-of-the-box sidekick, I would tell you 'yes'. Turns out we can learn a lot about ourselves and our friends if we better unpack these prototypes. Who are they? And, further, who are they within us?

Jewish wisdom provides interesting insights. Rabbi YY Jacobson notes that each Torah personality we read about represents an individual that lived but also a timeless characteristic that exists within every human personality. In the case of two sisters who are destined to become wives of the patriarch, Jacob, these two represent two very different distinct aspects of the human psyche.

CONSCIOUS AND UNCONSCIOUS

Leah, the elder sister, corresponds to the unconscious and deeply internal aspects of self, those aspects that necessarily defy expression in words. Jacob was tricked into marrying Leah. She was the rejected wife, deeply sensitive and perceptive, she suffered the ills of the world more acutely, was more subject to tears.

The Torah describes her as having weak or dim eyes. Commentators note that she looked with deep intensity. She had that look of deep apperception, she saw to the core of situations and people. As a result, Leah suffered, she took things to heart.

Rachel, in contrast, was the woman Jacob wanted to marry. The name Rachel derives from the Hebrew word that corresponds to Ewe, a female sheep. Rachel was docile, peaceful, unperturbed. She was beautiful but not complicated. Rachel's gift was expression and mastery of the practical, predictable world. Socially gifted, a character that we easily understand, she is the master of pleasantries and fits in any environment, qualifies for any job, effortlessly masters the tasks the world would have her do. Rachel, we get.

The complicated, brooding Leah, always thinking, always analyzing, lives in a higher dimension. Constantly processing abstractions and values, she doesn't fit into our everyday paradigm. Society is more apt to reject Leah. And to celebrate Rachel.

In the Jewish vernacular, Rachel represents speech and Leah represents thought. Rachel is the master of the 'Revealed world', the social and concrete world, the stuff of everyday life. Leah is in touch with the 'Hidden world', a higher world. She is unconventional, the artist, the musician, the muse. And Leah only finds a home in the revealed world when she partners with Rachel. Hence the prototypical BFF partnership!

It's no coincidence that the Mary Tyler Moore Show centered around a pretty, personable, pleasant Mary Richards. It's no coincidence that Mary produced the news. The Mary in each of us is the speaker, the one who can explain, the one with the basic comprehension of that which is everyday and matter-of-fact. That show presented the Rachel prototype and introduced us to Leah.

Rhoda: brilliantly witty, rough around the edges, blurting out that which most would think but never think to say, coming up with ingenious insights and subject to constant rejection ("Hello. I'm the other person in the room.").

Long-suffering, Rhoda has a difficult time in the revealed world. Everything goes wrong! She doesn't find an easy home here! Or as Rhoda puts it, on the one day when Mary is in a funk and Rhoda is doing well:

"You're having a lousy streak. I happen to be having a terrific streak. Soon the world will be back to normal. Tomorrow you will meet a crown head of Europe and marry. I will have a fat attack, eat 3,000 peanut butter cups, and die."

When Rhoda graduates to her own show, she becomes the Rachel character and her sister, Brenda, is the new Leah, self-deprecating, consistently rejected.

On the other hand, being Leah is not all bad news. Our Leah character is always unabashedly herself. She doesn't succumb to social pressure. Leah represents the zone of internality. Such characters never lose the pulse of their own unique originality.

In contrast, the sages teach, the Rachel character can fall into exile, lose her voice, succumb to social pressure. In the Torah, Rachel represents the *Shechina*, the aspect of Divinity that has been exiled from this world. So the Rachel's of this world have their own problems. Too often, they lose their voice and stray from their truth, often in the context of relationship. They partly find themselves, though, in their pairing with Leah.

And so you have the prototypes: the zany creative and the beautiful ingénue. Each the master of their own domain. The two archetypes work marvelously as a team.

Look around. You'll often see this BFF pairing in the world at large. With every successful partnership, the two domains of the world, the hidden and the revealed, are better bridged. The Mary/Grace character is the master of competence and social convention. The Rhoda/Frankie character brings flavor, insight and novelty into the moment. Rachel is order. Leah has her finger on the pulse of that which is unknown, ephemeral or otherworldly. Leah is 'out there' but her perspective is fresh, interesting and important.

RACHEL AND LEAH WITHIN

Life is full of complexities; for the Rachel's and Leah's in the world; also for the ones we each find, within. The inner Rachel has mastered social mores but sometimes fails to access her own inner truth. The inner Leah houses your idiosyncrasies and aspects of self that are inaccessible, sometimes only channeled through art, poetry or via dreams at night. Rachel is your Sun. Leah is your Moon.

Our first reaction to Leah, whether the one within or the one in the world at large, is rejection. Rabbi Jacobson points out that we hate that which we don't understand. When someone or something is too deep, too incomprehensible, our first response is to deny it or delegitimize it. The inner Leah hosts aspects of the world that are unintelligible, confusing, even overwhelming. Let's put that differently: your Leah hosts aspects of *you* that are unintelligible, confusing, even overwhelming.

And yet, we *must* divine down more complex aspects of reality *and* ourselves. If we will sit with the Leah dimension, reject the urge to turn away, we will befriend imminent aspects of reality (and self) that will expand our lives and our paradigms. We will be better for it.

In fact, the more you integrate your own Leah, the more you can partner with the Leah dimension of your spouse. As Jordan Peterson would say, we have to master the domain of the familiar, but also extend a tendril into the unknown. We have to open to aspects of self and world that don't make sense. We have to figure them out. And escort them into our lives.

You only really get to marry Rachel – and have a life characterized by acceptance – when you marry Leah – first. And so you watch Mary and Rhoda or Frankie and Grace to get a whiff how one might achieve such an inter-inclusion. Watching the social dance between these two archetypes helps us architect and bring together the two prototypes we harbor within.

Long live our BFF's, connecting us to a landscape that is variable and complex, showing us how the other half lives and bringing us into deeper resonance . . . with ourselves!

REFERENCES

Poizner, Annette (2020). *"Knock, Knock": The Kabbalah of Comedy (The How, Why & What of Funny)*. Toronto: People of the Books, Ink.

Poizner, Annette (2020) *Kabbalah Café: Ancient Wisdom for Modern Minds*. Toronto: People of the Books, Ink.

ABOUT THE AUTHOR

Annette Poizner, MSW, Ed.D., RSW

Annette Poizner is a psychotherapist in private practice, a published author and community educator. She completed her Masters degree in Social Work at Columbia University of New York and a Doctorate in Education (specializing in Counseling Psychology) at the University of Toronto.

She has specialized training in techniques developed by Dr. Milton Erickson, as well as advanced training in the use of Eye Movement Desensitization Reprocessing (EMDR) and Neuro Linguistic Programming (NLP). She is the co-founder of the Milton H. Erickson Institute of Toronto. She has a strong interest in Jungian psychology and addresses archetypes within her clinical work with clients.

Her work had been featured in dailies across Canada, in trade magazines across North America, and in clinical and academic venues such as at the Canadian Psychological Association annual conference and other professional meetings. She is the author of a textbook published by a leading scholarly publishing house. "Clinical Graphology: An Interpretive Manual for Mental Health Practitioners." Among her volumes published under the Lobster University Press imprint are: A Practical Summary & Workbook for Using Jordan Peterson's Maps of Meaning to Sort Yourself Out, An Illustrated Guide to Using Jordan Peterson's Insights Regarding Divinity and the Map of Meaning to Sort Yourself Out, In Good Standing: Using Jordan Peterson's Insights on the Structure of Self to Sort Yourself Out, This Way Up: A Faith-Based Introduction to Jordan Peterson's Maps of Meaning , Clean Your Room: An Out-of-the-Box Manual for Lobsters and From Chaos to Order: A Guide to Jordan Peterson's Worldview. An upcoming volume is Yin, Yang & You: An Eastern Commentary on Jordan Peterson's 12 Rules for Life .

You can access more of her work on her blogs on the Times of Israel and Medium.com and her YouTube channel. To be advised of the release of the next book in this series or to contact her with feedback about this work (which will be sporadically updated) please email ap@annettepoizner.com.

The following pages provide more information about other educational coloring books in this series.

THE JORDAN PETERSON CHEAT SHEET

"Pursue what is meaningful, not what is expedient"

A collection of Jordan Peterson quotes and images for coloring

THE JORDAN PETERSON CHEAT SHEET: THE COLORING BOOK THAT CAN CHANGE YOUR LIFE!
"A picture tells a thousand words"

Many can benefit from the pearls that Jordan Peterson shares and many have found incredible inspiration in his teachings, but not everyone will tune in to lengthy lectures. If you have been heartened by Peterson's work and looking for a modality that might capture the interest of someone you know, this may be the right gift!

Peterson describes a hallmark of truth, saying "it snaps things together....You have a nature, and when you feel that nature articulated, it's like the act of snapping the puzzle pieces together." In this work, the goal is to facilitate that type of revelation, by pairing compelling quotations with visual images which can then be colored! Using humor, word play and creative visual renderings, this work will unlock insight into self and other, detonating truth bombs that let readers peek into the infrastructure of reality and access some of the fascinating insights that underpin Jordan Peterson's worldview. In a resource designed to inspire growth, learning - and a cleaner room - the author provides an inroad, allowing readers to access teachings that have, to date, catalyzed many.

Coloring books allow readers to reflect and focus, building concentration skills, this in an age characterized by distraction, busyness and skimming. The coloring book modality is designed to bring quiet back into life. As a modality, it also reinforces Peterson's message: 'what if you attended to each detail in your life like it mattered. Imagine what that outcome would look like!'

Once introduced to memorable quotes and concepts, readers can follow up by watching Peterson's lectures. Additional journaling pages are provided for those who further explore Peterson's work to curate content, recording quotes as they come upon them.

Annette Poizner, MSW, Ed.D., is a clinical social worker, therapist and community educator who has written extensively on the work and worldview of Dr. Jordan B. Peterson. Among the books she has written about the work of Jordan Peterson is Finding One Self: A Teenager's Guide to Jordan Peterson's Rules for Life. That book provides young readers with an accessible treatment of many of the rules that Peterson discusses.

Lobster University Press, publishes short volumes which unpack ideas introduced by Dr. Jordan Peterson in his talks and books. The materials published are designed to help people better integrate the material and tweak that most important of abilities: the capacity to "turn chaos into habitable order!" These works will be the product of discourse and exchange with others interested in Peterson's work, as we continue to mine the depth of his opus and explore interesting and helpful applications.

INNER NATURE

A Carl Jung Coloring Book

for Self-Exploration

Volume 2 of Jung@heart

Made in the USA
Middletown, DE
17 November 2023

42963293R00084